MISSION MARS

Written by Anne Curtis

Illustrated by Chris Corner

Collins

Star Ship Orca.
Mission: to find a new planet
for the people of Earth.

10 - 9 - 8 - 7 - 6 - 5 - 4 - 3 - 2 - 1

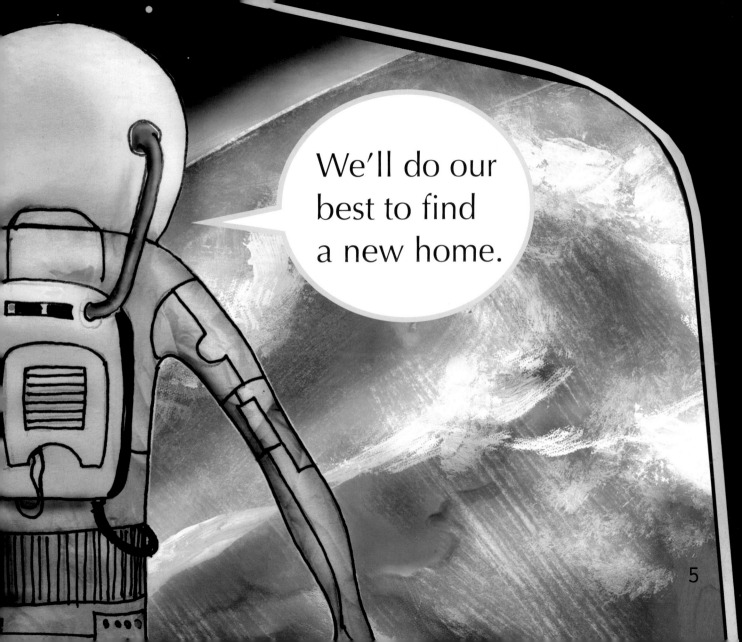

The crew check SS Orca before they leave the Moon's orbit.

6

The SS Orca heads towards Mars.

8

Star Ship Orca's journey

Ideas for reading

Written by Gillian Howell
Primary Literacy Consultant

Learning objectives: *(reading objectives correspond with Yellow band; all other objectives correspond with Copper band)* use phonics to read unknown or difficult words; empathise with characters and debate moral dilemmas portrayed in texts; present events and characters through dialogue to engage the interest of an audience; use layout, format, graphics, illustrations for different purposes

Curriculum links: Science: Light and shadows

High interest words: to, a, new, for, the, people, of, we, have, off, our, in, your, last, good, do, home, all, now, on, there, no, live, here, but, look, been, and

Interest words: mission, people, Earth, planet, future, Moon, Mars, touchdown, friends

Resources: paper, pens, pencils, internet

Word count: 89

Getting started

- Read the title together. Ask the children what they know about space travel and the planets, including Mars. Point out the *ss* has a *sh* sound in *mission*. Ask the children what sort of text they think this is (Science fiction).

- Turn to the back cover and read the blurb together. Ask the children if this will be a fiction or non-fiction book and give reasons for their

ideas. Ask them to flick briefly through the book to confirm their thoughts.

- Turn to p3 and point out the speech bubble. Check the children understand that this indicates spoken words. Ask them who they think is speaking here.

Reading and responding

- Ask the children to read the book aloud but in a quiet voice. Listen to the children as they read and prompt as necessary. Remind the children to use their phonics knowledge to work out new or difficult vocabulary.

- On p4, ask the children to point out the apostrophe in *future's* and *you're*. Ask them to say why an apostrophe is used and to say the full phrase *future is*. Ask them to look out for other contracted verb phrases as they read.

- At p9, stop and ask the children to predict what they think the team might find on Mars, then continue reading to see if they were correct.

- Occasionally pause and ask the children to say who they think is speaking the dialogue in the speech bubbles and practise reading with expression.